# Also by Artress Bethany White

### Poetry
*My Afmerica*
*Fast Fat Girls in Pink Hot Pants*

### Prose
*Survivor's Guilt: Essays on Race and American Identity*

### Coedited
*Wheatley at 250: Black Women Poets Re-imagine
the Verse of Phillis Wheatley Peters*

# A BLACK DOE
# IN THE ANTHROPOCENE

Recd 6th November 1777 of Mr. Peter Hairstone One hundre
& one pounds Current money, for a Negro Wench & Child
For Mrs Mary Byrd
Jerman Baker

# A BLACK DOE IN THE ANTHROPOCENE

POEMS

## ARTRESS BETHANY WHITE
Foreword by Barbara McCaskill

*A note to the reader:* The poems in this volume employ sensitive language to describe historical and contemporary instances of oppression and violence. Discretion is advised.

Copyright © 2025 by Artress Bethany White

Published by The University Press of Kentucky,
scholarly publisher for the Commonwealth, serving Bellarmine University, Berea College, Centre College of Kentucky, Eastern Kentucky University, The Filson Historical Society, Georgetown College, Kentucky Historical Society, Kentucky State University, Morehead State University, Murray State University, Northern Kentucky University, Spalding University, Transylvania University, University of Kentucky, University of Louisville, University of Pikeville, and Western Kentucky University.
All rights reserved.

*Editorial and Sales Offices:* The University Press of Kentucky
663 South Limestone Street, Lexington, Kentucky 40508-4008
www.kentuckypress.com

*Frontispiece:* Wilson and Hairston Family Papers #04134, Southern Historical Collection, Wilson Library, the University of North Carolina at Chapel Hill

Cataloging-in-Publication data is available from the Library of Congress.

ISBN 978-1-9859-0261-9 (hardcover : alk. paper)
ISBN 978-1-9859-0262-6 (paperback : alk. paper)
ISBN 978-1-9859-0264-0 (epub)
ISBN 978-1-9859-0263-3 (pdf)

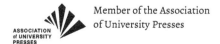

*In memory of an institution and its enduring legacy.*

# Contents

Foreword by Barbara McCaskill   ix

The Saura of Stokes County, North Carolina   1

**Original Sin**

A Family History   5

Oral Slave Narrative   6

An Extant Slave Receipt Signed *Peter Hairston*   7

Dear Ancestors: On the Occasion of Visiting the
Plantation Which Once Governed Your Lives   9

A Black Doe in the Anthropocene   11

Matrilineal   13

Racial Ambiguity   14

A Bondage Nocturne   15

Encroachment   19

Plantation Aubade: Freedom as Lover   20

Hemings Family Tour   21

When the Enslaved Dream   24

What I Will and Will Not Take from a Planter Ancestor   25

Crops: Tobacco   26

Bill of Sale 1832 December 21st   27

On the Occasion of Enumeration   28

A Creased Page from a Hairston Plantation Ledger   30

Pancakes Keep Coming to Mind: A Sestina Commemorating
the Demise of Aunt Jemima on the Pancake Box   32

Runners: A Ghazal for Our Times   34

Runaway Slave Affidavit Dated March 1831   35

Paul, Where You Going to Run To?   36

Resurrection 37

George's Dilemma, Anno Domini 1777 38

Of Bison and Bullets: A Preservation Project 39

My Father Singing "John Henry" 42

The Negro Girl Letter 43

Dear [Negro] Body 44

Every Day Can Be Resistance 45

Esclave/Schiava/Escrava/Slave 46

## Back to Africa

Severed: A Statement on the Ludicrous Nature of African Repatriation 49

Notebook of a Return to Africa: Accra, Ghana 50

Elmina [Slave] Castle: Est. 1482 53

The Vanishing 54

Homegoing to Africa as Ars Poetica 55

The Origins of an "Americo" in Liberia 57

Vibrio Cholerae 58

The Good Ship *Jupiter* 59

Sherbro, West Africa 60

## Home Again

Reconstruction 65

Just in Case They Change Their Minds, Let My Epitaph Read, *Free* 66

Up from Slavery 68

A Meditation on the Toppling of the Confederate Statue *Silent Sam* 69

Slivers 70

## Afterword

My African American Sensibility Speaks to My Scottish
Genes about the Miniseries *Outlander* 75

Acknowledgments 77

Notes 79

About the Author 85

# Foreword

Well, what was more American than this?
—Artress Bethany White, "A Creased Page from a
Hairston Plantation Ledger"

During the mid-nineteenth-century height of the genre in the United States and the British Isles, a best-selling narrative of enslavement was Harriet A. Jacobs's *Incidents in the Life of a Slave Girl: Written by Herself*. First published in Boston in 1861, the book was released in London the following year with the conspicuous title *The Deeper Wrong*. In both editions, Jacobs wrote using the pseudonym Linda Brent to recount her true, terrifying history as a young Black woman enslaved and tormented by a sexually predatory white doctor and his bitter, sadistic, nominally Christian wife. Jacobs's racially mixed blood and flesh already embodied the rape of Black women by the white men who enslaved them. To defy the power of one white man, she reluctantly consented to bear the children of another.

The bodies and blood of such Black women, enslaved or free, assertive or constrained, fortify the personal and collective stories that Artress Bethany White shares in *A Black Doe in the Anthropocene*. Her family's epic progress from the eighteenth century, as Black people enslaved in a Highland immigrant's "plantation empire" ("A Family History"), through her own twenty-first-century reunion with the West African motherland ("Notebook of a Return to Africa"), is magnificently signposted in the three sections of this volume by the bodies, voices, images, and aspirations of such Black women, and by those of their husbands, fathers, lovers, sons, and other male kith and

*ix*

kin, distant and close. In her endnote about her poem "A Bondage Nocturne," White remarks that even the harrowing testimonies of enslaved Black women's bildungsromans like Jacobs's insufficiently prepared her for the normalized rape and molestation of Black teen girls she encountered while searching for records of her own ancestors in bondage.

The poems of *A Black Doe in the Anthropocene* record slavery's indecencies, Jim Crow's individual humiliations and collective violence, and the nation's pantomime of reconciliation and healing during the post-Obama years of racial reckoning, when "protests now [bloomed] viral after Black / bodies [were] rendered fallow" ("Resurrection"). The collection defiantly envisions arms and aspirations stretching out toward Africa, a post–racial backlash America, and a place yet to be identified where a Black sister's multiple racial and cultural identities are not held either against her or in tension; she can choose relationships "based on consent, not rape" ("Hemings Family Tour"); and there is "one less sun-glazed statue to climb," as White reflects in her meditation on the toppling of the University of North Carolina at Chapel Hill's *Silent Sam*. A perspicacious metaphor from this poem that coheres the collection into a single narrative is the notion of American history as "collective whiplash." The long arc of history that connects these poems does not incline toward justice for African-descended people. It repeats bitter lessons of separation, disenfranchisement, and unrealized citizenship, even as it sustains the promises of community, freedom, unrestricted access to the ballot, and other civil liberties.

When Black women appear in White's poems, they are not hypersexualized or hapless. They are complicated figures whom we admire in spite of their failures. Rocketing across time and place on these pages, they display intense emotions and buoyant spirits. White bears witness in Accra, for example, to "a veiled girl hawking shoeshines" whose "giddiness and sass [are] all on view" and are at variance with media stereotypes of Muslim women who wear hijabs and burkas as

*x*

being cowed into silence and submission ("Notebook of a Return to Africa"). A Black man who, like White's great-grandfather, was born into bondage, carries himself and his family "Up from Slavery" and through the hate and violence that follows by wearing a respectable uniform of "coat, tie, and well-worn shoes." This is an armor of affability that enables him "to stay alive" in a culture where looking at or speaking to white people out of turn, or building wealth that attracts their envy, can be fatal.

Like the slave ship that transported White's African ancestors to America; the pre-Emancipation ship that transported a group of Black Hairstons to Monrovia, Liberia; and the railroad lines that have carried other Black people to and from the South in modern migrations and reverse migrations, White's poems shuttle back and forth across time and topographies. Her poems are asynchronous memories "forever refusing / alignment, beginning, ending, or arc" ("Dear Ancestors") and eschewing chronological order. Their nonlinear arrangement mimics physical, linguistic, religious, and cultural dislocations, coerced and involuntary, that have scarred but not broken her biological and fictive kin. She counters this turbulence and rupture with a comforting, recurring, quintessentially American nostalgia for home. This theme of home has been elusive and shifting, an uncashed "promissory note"—to quote Dr. Martin Luther King Jr.'s famous speech—for America's Black citizens.

White's book offers her own family genealogy as evidence of Black history's "oral tapestry, / spooled into ears like unwoven kente" ("The Vanishing"). By speaking these stories aloud and committing them to paper in a way that recalls the haunted, admonitory refrain of Lucille Clifton's masterpiece "at the cemetery, walnut grove plantation," White does not so much uncover facts and ratify truths as she models to readers that "master narratives make race serendipitous" over time ("The Vanishing"). She makes visible how the narratives of European Americans who have bought, sold, and controlled Black bodies have intentionally erased, lied about, omitted, falsified, aided and abetted,

*xi*

and blurred and blotted out damning realities about white supremacy and racial genocide. As an archaeologist of the written word and an interpreter of the unsaid, White recovers and speaks aloud the ironies and secrets that have belied the written record, or what she describes as "the letters and shackled names / the bloated body of words on the page" of Black Americans' history in the United States ("Matrilineal"). A plantation ledger, a property roll, a slave's testimony, a receipt, an affidavit, a bill of sale, a census enumeration, a bill of manumission—all this parchment and paper confers legibility, form, and meaning to White's poems.

*A Black Doe in the Anthropocene* stitches together select lines and verses in the shapes of columns, letters, or receipts, signed and inscribed and ink blotched by white Americans who were literate to monetize and objectify those who were not. They evoke a call-and-response between the powerful and the oppressed, the propertied and the dispossessed, that calls into question the seeming objectivity or neutrality of the original documents that inspired them. As in the blackout poems and found poems of Tracy K. Smith (*Wade in the Water*, Graywolf Press, 2019) and Layli Long Soldier (*Whereas*, Graywolf Press, 2017), the manipulation and rearrangement of the language and structure of archival documents in White's work foregrounds how the narratives of Africans kidnapped to North America, and their progeny, too, have often been written out of history or into historical fabrications. They foreground how such appropriations have skewered Black subjects' humanity, warped our dignity, and imposed an enduring, multigenerational torment that has inflicted more anguish than the whips, collars, chains, and deadly diseases of enslavement.

"Every day can't be rebellion but will be resistance," one of White's speakers explains ("Every Day Can Be Resistance"). *A Black Doe in the Anthropocene* unites African Diasporic people globally in their experiences of oppression and resistance that began with the transatlantic slave trade and continue through the twenty-first century's crises of human trafficking and enslavement of migrant workers. Wrenching images of the physical pain and emotional anxiety that White's family members suffered because of overwork, microaggressions, and sexual and economic exploitation remind us of the unfair toll exacted on those who struggle under racial and class hierarchies. White juxtaposes forms associated with lovers and loving, such as the ghazal, nocturne, and aubade, with brutal content that contradicts the forms' traditional themes. The resulting contrast between joy and sorrow animates *A Black Doe in the Anthropocene* with the blues' resilient mandate to laugh in the face of suffering and plot forward momentum even while taking the proverbial two steps back. White dedicates this book to the institution of slavery that gave birth to the blues, and to slavery's "enduring legacy." Like Harriet A. Jacobs, who encountered in the North familiar, if subtler, versions of racism and race prejudice when she finally escaped to freedom, outsiderness and unbelonging unceasingly bedevil White's speakers and subjects. In spite of these burdens, as White's ancestral story exemplifies, what has not waned, but has often grown stronger, is her family's and her people's persistence and success in inventing consequential, creative lives and producing nurturing homes and institutions.

Barbara McCaskill

Barbara McCaskill is professor of English at the University of Georgia and associate academic director of the Willson Center for Humanities and Arts. She coedited *Post-Bellum, Pre-Harlem: African American Literature and Culture, 1877–1919* (NYU Press), cowrote *The Magnificent Reverend Peter Thomas Stanford, Transatlantic Reformer and Race Man* (University of Georgia Press), and authored *Love, Liberation, and Escaping Slavery: William and Ellen Craft in Cultural Memory* (University of Georgia Press). She serves as codirector of The Genius of Phillis Wheatley Peters: A Poet and Her Legacies, and of Culture and Community at the Penn Center National Historic Landmark District, funded by the Mellon Foundation.

*xiii*

# The Saura of Stokes County, North Carolina

For the Saura Indians, 1670 was the beginning of the end.
  —*Greensboro News & Record*

Before sorrow, there were no diseases

carried by settlers on southern breezes

to cull a people, winnow thousands to hundreds,

and birth fear of communal extinction.

Before sorrow, there was no sign stating,

*Upper Saura Town, A village of the Saura*

*. . . abandoned by that tribe* in the early 1700s,

making me stop and think about first feet

to sift needled pine until settlers

from those British Isles

ushered in the Saura's disease-ridden demise.

Before sorrow, there was no ritual

of living with the dead because it was said

they died too swiftly from an enemy

groomed a pearled ocean away.

Sorrow is a corpse bound and held close

with breathless hope; a lost people,

a broken homonym.

# Original Sin

It is to them I raise my song,
Thou land of blood, and crime, and wrong.
    —James M. Whitfield, "America"

The slave girl is reared in an atmosphere of licentiousness and fear. The lash and the foul talk of her master and his sons are her teachers. When she is fourteen or fifteen, her owner, or his sons, or the overseer, or perhaps all of them, begin to bribe her with presents. If these fail to accomplish their purpose, she is whipped or starved into submission to their will.
    —Harriet A. Jacobs, *Incidents in the Life of a Slave Girl: Written by Herself*

# A Family History

(In the 1700s, a Scottish immigrant)
~~made his way to the shores of British America~~
~~and~~ (began) ~~the process of~~ (purchasing)
~~land and slaves, to build~~ (a plantation empire).
(This family), ~~with the surname~~ (Hairston),
~~would establish a practice of their slaves not~~
~~regularly being sold outside the family.~~
~~As a result,~~ (both white and Black)
~~members of the family,~~ (in name and blood),
~~would remain~~ (tied) ~~to each other~~ (for generations).
[T]he great-granddaughter, (a descendant of Black
and white) ~~Hairstons~~ (weaves the story)
~~of her enslaved ancestors as it was~~ (passed down)
~~to her~~ (orally and through the plantation)
~~archives and vital records~~ (in poems).

# Oral Slave Narrative

When she said, *My grandfather,*
*your great-grandfather,*
*was seventy-five percent white,*
it was with an awe
reserved for feats of science,
not economic avarice
or slavery's salacious greed
making bodies to sell bodies
that looked damn near free.
When I was told, *His father*
*was his master, his mother a slave,*
while unsure how babies were made,
my child's mind birthed
Mary and Jesus miracles,
seeing plantations as living bibles
of unspeakable carnal deeds.
No Middle Passage and no Africa
just benevolent European fathers
chaste Black mothers
and acres upon acres of sorrow.

# An Extant Slave Receipt
# Signed *Peter Hairston*

*1777*

*Negro wench and child*, declares the receipt,
Black woman, I mentally retaliate.

In Europe, a royal wench was dubbed a lady,
not a metonym for social promiscuity.

Consider the barmaid—much like cook,
except a few beers and coin most certainly could

turn a hardworking one to lusty wench,
only daylight morphing her to maid again.

The price of *Two hundred & one pounds* on American
soil turned this Black woman to wench in no time at all,

and what happened between her thighs, resulting in a child,
made it a two for one: some planter's coy prize.

I want to divine her name and that of her babe,
know much more than this receipt entails.

It is not enough that the sweat of the planter seller
is mixing with the DNA of my fingertips

as his genetic code resides within me.
My inheritance the oft-turned phrase

*This family had a habit of not selling off their slaves*
and so many receipts neatly tucked away.

# Dear Ancestors
## On the Occasion of Visiting the Plantation Which Once Governed Your Lives

*Davie County, North Carolina, Summer 2021*

Four generations past calling anyone master
and this word alone would make you spin
in a grave, enraged gyre at the promise, threatened
but not broken, to never see your children's children
bound and beholden to any man, woman, or soil
once calling them slave.

Free, I see more than you thought would endure
amid Piedmont pines and plantation shrines.
Driving to Cooleemee on Peter Hairston Road,
a new gated walk to bar my way, I realize
more than one tourist gathers here today
when a family thrusts a ten-year-old child my way.
*My forebears once worked this land*, I say.
They call it luck and serendipity
and rush to arrange a photo op including me.

I become the project on the Civil War,
a book holding the names of my family
as property gripped in a child's freckled arm.
I wonder how the school report will go,
after a panicked look when I utter

*9*

*I was a blood relative of the planter, you know,*
not just chattel abiding in slave quarters
gathered round this stately manor.

Soon enough I am glad to leave behind
the touristy tangle of cotton vine
at the end of that rutted, mile-long drive.
The bump of roadkill beneath my wheels,
I pass a flagpole three banners deep,
American, Confederate, and Trump
emblazoned on blue declare what
you already knew: healing this
generation's troubles is long overdue.

O, America, you are such a dreamer.
I am related to a nineteenth-century man
who took a Black "wife" and whose
descendants would go on to be enslaved
for life, to have and to hold till narratives
do us part, fragments forever refusing
alignment, beginning, ending, or arc.

# A Black Doe in the Anthropocene

*after the mass shootings in Buffalo and Uvalde*

I only wanted to see the plantation where my
forebears trod, place my feet in the footprints
of enslaved lives. *Let's just walk through
the woods to see it* I said, in a flash forgetting
the nature of guns and people in towns
where weapons are primed in every room,
under pillows, in picture frames
beyond the limpid gaze of a pair of deer eyes.

Forgetting as soon as my sneakers
sifted needled pine I would become
a black doe in the Anthropocene
fighting to see without being seen.

And when the landowner appeared
in a black pickup truck draped in camo
to defend his property, I felt the "ask"
of a peek at manor history
die in my chest like payback unpaid.

What is it about camouflage and tactical
gear that recalls white sheets and a
deadly sneer?

*11*

Television tries to woo with pain
but there is no romance in the sound
of a body hitting the floor
or children crying behind a closed door.
No intellect in the mechanics of a gun,
or two young men counting bodies
making life a video game for fun.
The only prize here, their own demise,
tok tik with nothing to remit.

A high school and college dropout
stealing grandmothers, grandfathers,
children, and dreams. Then a boy
pauses to tell me young men now think
college is a waste of time, and my mind
screams, and screams, and screams.

My ancestors lived through the Middle Passage
the breeding of their bodies and the crack
of cowhide. Were weaned on seeing
their own mothers' breasts in the
mouths of children who didn't drop
from between their raised brown knees.

Swallowed venom clogging their throats
mingled with dust under burning suns
and now students can't study the pages
of race history, our only survival legacy.
If ancestors were here today speaking truth
to this murderous shame, the words would
roll through the trees and over the plains:
*Behold the lilies, throw down the guns,*
*Behold the lilies, throw down the guns.*

*12*

# Matrilineal

I think about my mother tied by blood
swirling me in racial taxonomies
wanting nothing to do with slavery.

Her love of Disney over planter tableau
technicolor bright with a catchy beat.
Contemplate my mother knotted by blood

heard tap-tapping through plantation pages
heir to red hair, freckled skin, Scottish genes,
who will have nothing to do with slavery.

Fate is African and Euro lineage,
set on a ship's route, cargo and steerage.
I think about my mother's fettered blood

from childhood our genealogy parsed
to ensure memory by a woman
wanting nothing to do with slavery.

I have seen the letters and shackled names
the bloated body of words on the page.
I consider my mother tied by blood
whose body screams of slave history.

*13*

# Racial Ambiguity

*Circa 1960s*

When I imagine my parents driving South
I think of the film *Green Book*, Doc Shirley
my dad, mom the gruff Italian driver.

There are shades of difference, but not color.
Dad claims they were never stopped on a hunch,
driving swampy byways coupled in the South

despite her looking lighter after dark.
When they took flight to make Georgia by midnight,
my Black dad driving my non-Sicilian mother,

I imagine a vigilant Dixie
prepared to arrest or exile them both
for tooling across Southern racial lines.

I'm sure police who spied them clearly believed
my Afroed pop would not stupidly test
a Neapolitan Miss Daisy at the wheel,

wife or not, to spell him in the time of
John, Robert, Medgar, Martin, and Malcolm
the perils of the South too imaginable
with her looking more Italian than not.

# A Bondage Nocturne

*I.*

In darkness / empirical evidence underhand /
a fingertip rubs black / but not ink.
A porcelain doll / he squints and thinks /
drags a thumb across yellow Scottish teeth.
A tug of war / with ownership rites. /
A girl fears a feral man / who talks
abed narration / whispering *temptress* /
while her eyes stammer back *neophyte*.

While her eyes stammer back *neophyte* /
[he] whispers *temptress*. / Talks
abed narration. / A girl fears a feral man /
with ownership rites / a tug-of-war
under yellow Scottish overbite. /
Dragging a thumb / he squints and thinks /
a porcelain doll black / but not ink. /
A fingertip rubs / empirical evidence
underhand / in darkness.

*II.*

A chill pricks my heart when I read the name
of the third enslaved girl to bear a child at age fifteen,
conception like clockwork proclaimed.
Some gossip to blame for declaring first blood,
ovulation oblique invitation on the plantation.

I pause to record the names of the nascent enslaved
and the many who have since taken the bodies of Black women,
bending them to the will of money, science, nothing.
A soul and body dubbed commodity, chattel, property.

I learned something of this game
in a basement to an Isley Brothers jam,
no warning beyond *Would you like to dance?*,
then hardness ground into a hip
beneath some dude's double knits.
Wanting to run but pinned by a palm holding mine
in a roomful of swaying bodies and sweat shine
until the prayed-for-end to that innocence-usurping time.

Something's cooking in the kitchen and in the fields,
it's bubbling up babies, sun scorching brow and hands.
Pick me a wonder, pick me a dream, how many hands
does it take to make heaven, a dearth of freedom
in this godforsaken land.

*III.*

The stomachs of daughters erupt
like burls on stalky trees.
Within a body, a sacred whorl curls;
outside it, a kettle whistles steam.

> *You branched her where I could not reach*
> *crossed good to annex evil*
> *while I still parted hair for braids,*
> *plowing lines from nape to brow.*

Chills shake a slave mother's heart
for what happens beyond her gaze.
Her girl fourteen, "Yellow" Milly fifteen,
singled out under the planter's mien.
"To mulatto," *verb*: a ritual distillation
removing color and taint
from plantation bait,
budding yet another beige slave.

*IV.*

What did she think . . .
when she eyed the enslaved women around her
whose bellies swelled beneath expectant palms
and bound fathers dropped kisses on cheeks at sundown,
skin still tight with the brine of sweat in the pre-moonlight.

What did she think . . .
on the way back to cabin quarters
of these same men and women bearing bondage together
whispering freedom prayers over a womb's bloom
placental incubator of protest and rebellion.

What did she think . . .
When whiskey-tinged breath called her name
from across the road separating girlhood from mother,
slave cabin from plantation house, and timid girl from master.

What did she think . . .
when she named her pallid child after the only slave
who purchased his and his family's freedom
before leaving the walls of Cooleemee Plantation.

# Encroachment

Rage from a white woman toward a Black
Screams *This body just won't do*
the words *But I once owned you*
history articulating a time
when Africans were a hostile mistress' wealth
a guaranteed come up
from being property herself
of a husband who had a choice
of whose legs he split in stealth.
There is nothing more despised
than a sister at ease in her own skin
the hard-won swagger before a predator's desire
to drape it over pale arms gaudy and feral.
I know this to be true because I heard a Karen once claim
*You move so comfortable* *within your skin*
as if she wanted to peel me to see what lay within
that *comfort* that *movement,*
that othered self.

# Plantation Aubade
Freedom as Lover

When the quiet fingers of dawn
barely pick at the night-dark sky
and neither lash, nor striking hand,
nor bark of words
strafe my body
just there,
like the hard-won
meat of fall's pecans,
the soul petals at dawn,
reaches back to what it once knew
before being penned to another's dream:
house and field bearing your blood but never your name.
Dear freedom, sweet companion, rising beneath my tongue,
I press lips against escape, already imagining the crepuscular
    morn.

# Hemings Family Tour

*Charlottesville, Virginia, 2019*

*I.*

Peering over Monticello's lawns,
a founding father's pillared roost,
I tour the layers of history,
passing from room to room.
Pedophile. Master.
A conflation of ego and blood.

*I brought my daughters here*
*To learn about slave history.*
Her oldest, a lithe fourteen,
same age as Sally when Jefferson made
her name synonymous with sex slavery.

Dawn mist parts beneath chattel tread.
To field, to weave, to blacksmith.
Even the trees rustle a sly rebuke—
*What God alone inhaled,*
*greed choked out in servitude.*

*II.*

I listen to the guide parse
Jeffersonian genealogy.
*House slave, field slave; a slave*
*by any other name, still a slave.*
When he narrows his gaze on me
stating, *I will never understand*
*how you feel about this history,* I want to say
*Dude, you are the same beige as my mother;*
*I thought you were Black like me.*

*III.*

Leaving Charlottesville, my stepdaughter
leans in, asks if her new mixed cousin
will be light or darker than she,
signifying even biraciality
has its own hierarchy. I do not say
one of you can pass, the other cannot.

Color soon forgotten, the two cavort
like fish at play around the aquarium
on this bright, summer day.

Niece, a sweet surprise, finds time
to hug my waist and grab my hand,
whispering, *You look like my mother.*
She does not, however, resemble my sister
save her quick temper and eyes; otherwise,
she is her own pale jawline and blonde hair shine.

My mother has spent her life telling
the tale of our historical miscegeny,
Gayl Jones style, a circular litany.
And now we have as many European
men in our family producing children
as there were during slavery.
No judgment here.
Each relationship based on consent, not rape.
Our new history, a much cleaner slate.

# When the Enslaved Dream

it's within the eye of a hurricane of hurts
beating out the heart's tympani.
O sour taste of a thousand noes
linked to memories of home
the last trace gleaned
from the sweat-sheened
ovaled into a ship's keel
appended to refuse
making maggots sing.
A spiked thorn enters a bare foot
stumbling to walk upright
after flight
a woman's free
intake of breath
before the leaden
choke: a chain.

# What I Will and Will Not Take from a Planter Ancestor

Hairston.

I will have the name      because it came

by way of blood      and stripe.

Cowhide-split skin      and parchment script

the tearful separation      of kin from ship.

Prized receipt of sale      placed on a shelf

and the quartered body      in a cabin

or under an attic roof

to be near at hand      as driver or cook.


I will leave behind      the self-righteous greed

birthed of the bend      and sway of tobacco leaves

& curséd wheat sheaves.

# Crops
Tobacco

hornworm hooked beneath
a lean green tobacco leaf
undulating

Black back bowed and stooped
swaying to pick that leafing
for dip, chew, and pipe

infant of commerce
nurtured, suckered foliage
lucred link in chain

tobacco, *'bacca*
backbreaking hallowed smoke
cook these hands, this body

the rhythm of days:
tobacco they once stripped, cured
now chew, and then spit.

# Bill of Sale 1832 December 21st

The 3 × 5 parchment slip blooms into a body
under my magnifying glass. Limbs, heart, mind,
locked in terms negro, servant, bond.
Slavery's sumptuous sums blood to ink on a crusty receipt.

Zach Wilson *26 or 27 years of age*
*sound & healthy* blinks over at me
from the auction block his plantation destiny.
Mouths *What I could have done* *with the $699 that purchased me.*

I reckon with the torn page provenance of the hapless
   enslaved
speaking of value yet devoid of the four letters
that could set a man F    R    E    E.

# On the Occasion of Enumeration

the enslaved line up as the sun beats down.
Make their way to the desk
set under a tree, where the man
with the ledger holds sway.
Settled on its broad expanse
a glass of water,
a pot of ink,
pages to spare.

Handwriting
            D   I   P   S

                  sweeps
                  and serifs.
I come to know the character of a man
through the indifferent shrug of his hand:
                D
                P
                C
                S . . .
or, was the clerk
given a table in a room
on a lemon-scented floor,
his calculator's gaze summing up
each man, woman, and child
scraping soles before entering a back door.

Logic unfurled              he wrings a sea of names
roll call of the enslaved   carefully from his pen.
I see red                   decipher black ink limn
    ancestry
the stoicism of generations again and again.

The eyes that hunger, roll up to sample grandeur
mumble a name, before brusquely escorted to the field again.

# A Creased Page from a Hairston Plantation Ledger

*Chapel Hill, North Carolina, 2018*

Today I sift through the names of thirty enslaved
and pause over the sum of $1,000
to see what I imagine a planter might see:
a Black man full of genetic seed
and future saleable progeny.
No wait, it's the price of *John[s] Daughter*,
zeros now plain as lust's desire.
I record each name, history's syllabic lathe, cutting me.
When I get to *Dolly $600*, I see a chubby-cheeked woman—
can cook like nobody's business. When the prices drop
to $100 or so, I see old age. *Pleasant $325*
is named like an epiphany. *Citizen $600*,
a bad joke or history's irony.
*Sam $650, Lizzy $600*, and *Aggy $650*
suddenly proclaim gender equity.
Provenance accounts for something, I think,
when I see *Bill Bradley $850*. Not everyone
has this last name or a price so high;
it may be literacy or some other skilled pedigree.
I sadden over *Cecilia $175*—old now,
once a maid to her mistress in the early days,
when this colony was new for everyone.

The bookkeeper's pen struggled on the *g* in *Agnes $400*,
the ovaled top of this single letter bowed
like her head before him. *America Perkins $600*.
Well, what was more American than this?

# Pancakes Keep Coming to Mind
## A Sestina Commemorating the Demise
## of Aunt Jemima on the Pancake Box

*June 2020*

I invoke my great-great-grandmother's name on exhaled breath
the vowels arranging themselves in shorts and longs,
syntax and semantics duking it out.
Mima—that could have been birthed from an African tongue:
*Enee, meene, mima, mo,* respectable marriage of village,
continent, and town, without a diabolic *Je* like a pendulum swing

to the scarlet kerchief blooming in my brain, pancakes on my tongue,
unwilling to utter that name over Black families now living out
their American dream. Like reinvention, the heart longs
to reconcile past and present, within a village
raising a newer child clawing out of epicureal stink to swing
free from stereotypes, auction block, and Aunt Jemima's mealy breath.

Instead, pancakes every time my forebears' syllabics touch my tongue.
Mima sans *Je,* not *Meema,* or *Mi'ma[e],* coy notes stepping out
of a history where grits and flapjacks were birthed in a village
to skirt my teeth or strut 'cross my lips on exhaled breath,
that ample bosom and backside mocking me, she who longs
to rear up and bark *Breakfast!* and *Brunch!* on a revolving door swing.

*You are not my Auntie* or *Aunt* pronounced like the creature crawling out
over cadavers of supermarket boxes choking my breath
on a collapsed lung of shady marketing to keep bodies bound in a village-

cum-ghetto of stranger-than-strange imagined Black things, girl-on-a-swing
dreams culled from Western imaginings of what *that colored gal* longs
to do over a hot stove, flipping and flapping 'cause the griddle got her tongue.

Names as revenue monikers on revue, line dancing on a hip swing.
Oh, how daring to cogitate on destiny, each syllable a village
of preferred ubiquity, once the Ghanaian name *Afua* translated out
to first girl child born on a Friday, sonic genealogy on the tongue,
but changed to postbaptismal *Mary*, a rigid catechism of colonial breath
blowing across centuries of arid longing.

Food me, fooled me, sold me, told me, held me, bled me, tongue
afire with dreams of love, life, and freedom a profusion of days swinging
between something and more. My village compound, my village
quarters, my village a city block, each century censuring my breath.
What I seek is what I speak, not handed a script of nostalgic longing.
Jemima wrenched from shelves, but a litany in my brain still playing out.

Ain't nothing but a jonesing to tweak culinary history so my village
knows my branches are thick, swaying and swinging with longing and breath,
rolling descendancy off my tongue, blessing consumption out.

# Runners
## A Ghazal for Our Times

*for Ahmaud Arbery*

Frederick Douglass dashed without giving names—no shame,
certain more would follow his runner's game.

Our journeys cross at the Chesapeake Bay
waves lapping libation in that runner's game.

Harriet Jacobs fled gran's attic past Doc Flint's hands,
enslaved girl's tale of her own runner's game.

Sally Hemings's kin were freed under mama's gaze,
more akin to a mosey than a true runner's game.

Harken to dark days a continent away,
bodies stolen, shipped & stripped runner's game.

And now Artress born free while Ahmaud got treed,
white men in a pickup shouting, *Black criminal!* runner's game.

Ol' boys tout race pride, suck breath out Black hides,
make justice a running Black man's endgame.

# Runaway Slave Affidavit Dated March 1831

I Thomas Jones
being a justice of the peace
For the aforesaid county
do herby certify
that John R. Millner
of the county of Pittsylvania
Hath this day made oath before me,
That **Paul** a negroe slave
whom he had now Brought before me
is a runaway, that he
Has just grounds to believe
the said slave
is the property
of Robert Hairston of the county of Pittsylvania
that he was taken
upon the 17th day of March
in the year 1831 in the county of Pittsylvania
at the house of Richard Millner
and the distance, in my opinion,
between the said place where
the said slave was apprehended
and the plantation from which he fled
is five miles given under my hand this
18th day of March 1831

Thomas Jones

# Paul, Where You Going to Run To?

Lynchburg is small        and freedom scarce

      where we all look alike        until suddenly traced.

A runaway's price        barks at my heels

      in newer fields        where I saddle a horse

deliver a letter        or a cup of fresh water,

      respiration        stitching

my features at the fold        in a humble gaze lowered.

      Discovered        I calculate strides

beg desperate knees        to race for yonder trees.

*Nat Turner's Rebellion took place in Virginia in 1831.*
*Turner and a group of fellow enslaved persons*
*took the lives of over fifty people, including*
*planters and their family members.*

# Resurrection

What if Nat Turner's Rebellion had succeeded. Maybe he would
have birthed a trend, the way protests now bloom viral after Black
bodies are rendered fallow. Would people still root for a Nat
who craved more sumptuous fare, to be free sweet to his mind
like cane-cum-refined-sugar his ancestors once cultivated,
or the way a cotton shirt reminded his fingers of the pluck
of white bolls he hated. Today's revolt, to challenge a knee
on a neck where it's summarily planted or slow a bullet's trajectory,
John Woo style, before it lands. These thoughts rise up
like discontent-lined hymns to shorten bondage, planter eulogies
sown, hoed, and flowering amid sonorous darkness.
A love of Jesus grew Nat's courage skyward, a lofty sway
from bondage to freedom. To wit, one has to reap carefully
to glean the long-buried dead. Dismay mourns
the insurrections of the past while fearing
the bitter uprising never quite going down as planned.

*Henry County, Virginia*
*Upon the application of Peter Hairston for leave for his Negro*
*fellow to keep a gunn, leave & liberty is given & authorized*
*by me to said Negro fellow George to keep and make use*
*of a gunn, he in the meantime being of good behavior.*
*Given under my hand this 15th Dec. of 1777*
*—Edmund L.*

# George's Dilemma, Anno Domini 1777

Flintlock pistol or musket gun: master's choice.
Revolution places a gun in George's hand:
behavior a trusted slave's conundrum.

They say British freedom is pay for rebel heads,
if a Black man can fight and outlive a ball's lead.
Flintlock pistol or musket gun—gambler's choice.

A plucky bondsman could win his freedom now,
eschew loyalty's thankless pat on the brow,
behavior a trusted slave's conundrum.

Rumors rife of British moving southward,
a Virginia planter buys his empire slave by slave
while ol' massa puts a flintlock in George's hand.

Should he don a turncoat and run,
flee with the British across an ocean,
weapon cocked, slip the slave's conundrum?

A piece of parchment, a fragment of history
elides my rebel fantasy and St. George's reality.
Flintlock pistol or musket gun. Master's choice.
Good behavior or freedom: a conundrum.

# Of Bison and Bullets
A Preservation Project

*Golden Gate Park, San Francisco, California, 2022*

*for Jayland Walker*

Behemoths cleave to the landscape
like they have always been here
amid the care the preservationists exhibit
as they muck, monitor, and water.
Shaggy brown cloaks appear
more mange than majestic,
unlike the embossed portraits
on my father's hoard of buffalo nickels,
tossed carelessly into a dresser dish
alongside mismatched, popped buttons
and dulled copper pennies he called rare.
Did he know then that the species itself
was endangered, once not-so-rare victims
of overhunting by European settlers
committed to wanton western migration.
O the irony as I read
of conservation to replenish
the genus *Bison*, common name buffalo,
on Indigenous reservations
to restore glory to the family bovine,
the descendants of majestic herds
lured from the precipice of extinction.

I always confuse *preserve* and *reserve*,
to keep safe, to hide away
for now and tomorrow
on purpose for posterity.

Still, there is a parallel history
as our very communities become
preservation projects
harboring assault rifles
and teens programmed for defeat,
steered by parents who haven't
learned to parent yet.
I will not reserve judgment
as doctors help viewers digest
what a body looks like
after taking rapid rounds:
the severed heads

and eviscerated torsos abound.
Extinction. Has anyone had enough
of being enslaved by a trigger
aficionados can't let rest
ah, but I digress, they don't
want to preserve life
just reserve the right to shatter lives
and apologize in hindsight.
Let's try to preserve forty-eight bullets
pumped into the back
of a running Black man,
use the same handcuffs
that worked well to arrest
a twenty-one-year-old white man,
so they both can stand trial,
one for killing seven in Chicago

40

on the fourth of July
the other for killing absolutely no one.
Bison and bodies coalesce in my mind,
but this is muck work
for which no one seems to have the time.

# My Father Singing "John Henry"

*After Claudia Rankine*

I gleaned from John's tale, crooned at night,
a parable of being othered in the US:
work hard, beat the machine, then die a lyric epitaph.

History is full of stories of Black regret, Hetty's lament
in *The History of Mary Prince* as cowhide mapped her back:
*Oh, Massa! Massa! me dead. Massa! have mercy upon me—*
*don't kill me outright* while her heart murmured fervently,
salvage me instead, you devil, by your humanity tonight.

Another Black fragment torn from de Crèvecœur's *Letters*:
*I perceived a Negro, suspended in the cage and left there to expire!*
*I recollect . . . birds had already picked out his eyes*
truth of planned extinction amid too many national lies.

I found sweet dark love in James Baldwin's pages, a tutorial
on a soul kiss choreographed with passion
not reserved within a literary history best described
as 1,001 ways to disembowel Black lives.

# The Negro Girl Letter

Dear Peter Hairston
Sir,
I enclose you ten dollars towards paying
the expense & trouble of my sons Negro Girl,
I am sorry to find that the Girl
is likely to be a cripple,
she still walks very lame,
one leg shorter than the other
and seems to be turned one side,
I have no doubt but that the proper
attention was paid by yourself,
but there seems to have been
some bad management in setting the bone,
I am willing tho to do what you may think right
and I am anxious to give you satisfaction,
but am inclined [damage spot] when you learn
the situation of the Negro Girl
you will think the 20 dollars a high charge,
as I have no doubt
but she will be a cripple all her life,
but on this subject you must act
as you think right—
Yours Faithfully
Geremiah . . .
October 25th 1831

# Dear [Negro] Body
## A Reply from the Negro Girl to Her Ill-Used Person

*a tanka*

I, a rented hurt

float above you, landed fish

bones slaves could not knit

no verdant fields left to pick

undone, alone, recumbent

# Every Day Can Be Resistance

When I examine the portraits of the enslaved
the whole of freedom pauses for respiration
hands sifting soil                     abject frustration.
Every day can't be rebellion but will be resistance,
a man convinced that he is not a cow or horse
the way someone wants him        to mistake himself.
The hands of enslaved women like mitts, or
an old man's work hands years past labor,
still refusing balm
until fingers                          bowls of palms
crack, bleeding red lines like paper cuts in winter.
And so many women praying
unlike children with hands flat and fingers steepled
beneath raised chins,              but palms clasped,
fingers hugging, too swollen from work, chilblains, and arthritis
to ever lay flat                       unless broken.

*A Filipina migrant in Kuwait was killed by her*
*employers and found in a freezer more than a year later*
*—2018 Newswire story*

# Esclave/Schiava/Escrava/Slave

Shame is a boxed woman,
folded into a freezer.
Her new job a corpse
robbed of breath and destiny
save one reality:
in Kuwait a migrant maid
is no better than a slave.

In 2019 headlines scream
Africans are sold in modern-day Libya
with photos of black men folded into mesh cages
on a winding migration
from West Africa to the Mediterranean.
Once Muslim crusaders gave Africans Arabic names
*Abdul, Halim, Mamadou, Jabir, Ibrahim*
now holy brothers measure each other with disdain
unable to believe a blacker man
does not deserve to be his slave.

# Back to Africa

Go back to Africa!
—A slogan shouted by numerous young people of European descent throughout my childhood.

New facilities are daily offering to the scheme of getting rid of our coloured people, much to their own advantage as well as to ours.
—E. Ayers of the American Colonization Society (1824) advocates the virtues of African repatriation to end America's Negro problem

# Severed
## A Statement on the Ludicrous Nature of African Repatriation

*after a DNA test*

Twenty-four percent of my body should fly back to Mali,
heir to the legacy of Emperor Sundiata, Sogolon Djata,
whose mother's twisted body bore a great king
as prophesied by a griot to his father.

Four percent should be sculled back to Norway
aboard a historic Viking boat
to reunion with my Norwegian folk

Four percent should land in Portugal to satisfy genes
gained on an early slaving ship when the Portuguese
paved the way for English, Spanish, and Dutch
expansion of the transatlantic slave trade.

Forty percent should be removed to Angola
before tribal chiefs severed ties with their African brothers,
the spoils of domestic warfare sold to trader outsiders.

A final twenty-eight percent to the British Isles
a repatriation with Scottish, English, and Irish kin
to blame for this lighter skin
borne from centuries of blending in.

# Notebook of a Return to Africa
## Accra, Ghana

*for Sam Quainoo*

A glossary of power
graces Jubilee House,
the Ghanian president's abode,
draped with adinkra in filigreed gold:
a Black White House in an African nation,
a joyful excitation
in this new-to-me nation.

A veiled girl hawking shoeshines
captures the heart with joyful eyes.
I reach for five cedis to buy
a picture of youth
giddiness and sass all on view.
She throws up deuces
and leans into her swagger,
headscarf flapping and chipped
nail polish screeching *survivor*.

At night I watch young Ghanians sway
to Stonebwoy and Wendy Shay,
Afropop beats on a cloud of sinse,
and the children of the elite
sporting black Mercedes.
What I see when an Afroed child
drops it to the floor—the articulation

of hips surely to die for—is a community
where individuality is not policed
and where a sweet boy
can still stay sweet.

I think it will be the slave holds that shake
me to the core, but it's the stark realness
between the rich and poor. The street vendors
hawking anything they can,
the stench of aged aqueducts
fighting to be seen, and lean
people who eat unprocessed food
so really have no weight to gain.
I buy and buy, shedding money like cells
until the buying and selling
are finally quelled.

I am a *fufu* girl, not *banku*,
in the way I like my groundnut stew,
a lump at the bottom of my bowl
to easily scoop with fish and vegetable.
I fell in love with Ghanian spice
ate fish with *palava* at 9:00 am
to savor in my mouth.
The food always a win-win,
especially jollof with a side of plantain.

*J'ai un travail, avec les blancs.*
Diouana's singsong from beneath
a mask in *Black Girl* haunts
while mask shopping in sunny Accra.
*This belonged to my grandfather*
the seller claims,
proud to be a third-generation artisan.
I am not white but he still holds it tight
until the sale is final
tallying cedis, history, colonial grift,
and the mighty dollar
still holding the power.

My return to Ghana a corrective
to being ripped from its womb
by a system built on the ovaries
and backs of stolen African queens.
Generations fed on breasted milk
sipped between nascent lips
of enslaved babies and white planter free,
endless slavery vérité shadowing me.

I enter Elmina, a time warp severing me
from sisters and brothers crying *Akwaaba!*,
a toothsome *you are welcome*, arms held wide,
the one Twi word always uttered with pride.
I walk into the holding cells and palm rough walls,
assailed by a return awash in pained sobs.

*52*

# Elmina [Slave] Castle
## Est. 1482

*Cape Coast, Summer 2023*

At Elmina, the Ghanian guide says
*This is the well where women washed*
*before being taken to the mayor's door*
and my heart plunges into that dark,
an unhealed wound in a whitewashed tomb.
It is Bakatue—the festival for the merging
of two lagoons. Africa past and present
converge in this Portuguese fort
where fishermen still cast nets and sell wares
along meandering thoroughfares.
Elmina, final stop on the march from interior to coast,
dusty men, women, and children traded to parts unknown.
This could be the site of my ancestral embarkation,
that four percent of Portuguese blood
gathered here and distilled to me.

# The Vanishing

Disappearing blackness terrifies me.
Consider Thomas Commeraw, rendered white
until a census birthed his free and slave histories.

Master narratives make race serendipitous,
white blight hiding a diasporic legacy.
Is the act of vanishing color so titillating?

Colorblind curriculums, flawed politicians,
the devolution of race equity
an AI census unbirthing slavery?

Black freedom is still a cultural anomaly,
with archival data awaiting exhumation,
the terror of blackness boxed for extinction.

A potter's wheel churning out jars
became a life stashed away for eternity.
A tragic consensus; a slave birth suspended.

Black history once an oral tapestry,
spooled into ears like unwoven kente,
until census records birthed a black history,
vanished blackness this man's terrible destiny.

# Homegoing to Africa as Ars Poetica

*After Thomas W. Commeraw (1771–1823)*

The things we do in the name of art,
like stepping onto a ship now free and Black.
In 1820, Africa bound and innocent,
were you mistaken above deck or was the wind
calling *Com-mer-aw*, blotting from memory
a wife's spasmed shoulders braving brined troughs
and a fear that this return might be star-crossed.

Poetry is a series of lived and penned returns,
your story rich as palm oil pooling
red on a plate, a West African meal uneaten,
as wife Ann writhed in bedsheets,
losing a battle with malarial fever.

Royal blue glaze spelling *Commeraw*,
your name emblazoned on clay jars,
gray slip rimming your fingertips.
The jug's side the curve of a wife's hips,
a repeated recollection that weeps.

*Commeraw*, Africa talking to you
about a fresh start away from New York
and its hellish costs, to a nation full
of free Black men minus race hate.
*Commeraw* etched into eternity
despite a shattered dream and broken heart.

Sherbro Island, a misfired pot, wife now gone
after streaming regret as bitter
as a return to the country that once
enslaved you, this time fear of illness,
not chains, beating you back.

Despite this deserved return to US soil
a new headstone bearing your name,
*Thomas W. Commeraw*, by year's demise.

# The Origins of an "Americo" in Liberia

Like immigrants        made to assimilate
the enslaved were given        new names and mastered a tongue
so completely at odds        with where they came from.
Fully known        and appreciated by none,
what became        of some of this nation's sable sons?
Benevolence        a desire to do good toward one's fellows,
but repatriation        colonial folly, not *bon homme*,
when freed men and women        were placed on a boat
bound for Monrovia        in a Passage Middle roundabout.
They brought with them        their American clothes
and a white Jesus        previously unknown
to meet what missionaries called        "heathenish" ones.
They wanted        the middle-class life
threatened a continent away        and never
thought their African brethren        envisioned
lives a vastly different way.        So instead of being
Blacks among their own kin,        they became
*Americoes,*        despite the color of their skin,
alienated in a foreign land        once again.

*In 1830, amid a cholera epidemic, recently freed Hairstons*
*await passage to Liberia under the auspices*
*of the American Colonization Society.*

# Vibrio Cholerae

The face will turn as blue as an ocean
lips spew foul over a roiling stomach,
liquefy bowels no quick cure can slow.

How adjacent to death freedom can be,
the ship that would steer us to Africa
moored as cholera's death mask fills a city.

Sulky musings while stranded in Norfolk,
generations removed from shackles and chains,
and a ship's bowels full of waste-drenched slaves.

Port a cemetery of anchored boats,
every downcast visage a coy scythe raised,
and suspicion peaked by death's azure shades.

We idly drink cup after cup of tea
await solemn word of others stricken,
while nurses tend bowels doctors can't cure.

*Jupiter* waits, bound for Liberia
land my American feet never knew.
This face won't pitch as blue as an ocean;
my cure is freedom, bondage now over.

58

# The Good Ship *Jupiter*

There is wonder in a namesake. *Jupiter*,
colossus of ethereal majesty,
ringed body cast into celestial black.

Now, a wooden prow bobbing a brined sea
to eager grins of migrants eyeing tidal moon
with wonderous hope in the name of Jove.

Freedmen and freedwomen once plotted
bound for a continent in old *Oswego*'s hold,
ill-fated bodies soon winged and draped in black

the price of destiny beyond slavery's bitter grasp.
Imagine, brave enough to risk death by malaria
to escape America's Black strife.

There are so many ways to taste freedom:
by birth, manumission, buying back your own name,
a mother's dream residing in the ship *Jupiter*'s sail.

Thousands returned to Africa's west shore
to meet roots, their past, and future fates
riding presciently on Jupiter's namesake.
Brave Black bodies ringed in freedman's drape.

# Sherbro, West Africa

Colony, a conundrum of hope,
freedom planted amid slavery's roots.
How many steps beyond this weary boat
will it take to cut harbored dreams loose.

Ignore the sharp thrash of furious rain,
then sun's slouched blaze bathing eyes and brow.
The muscled ache of plans to build again
while mosquitoes needle to suck marrow.

Imagined I'd taste dirt like a woman
ripened with child and ravenous for birth
once landing safely, a workman ashore,
before sly starvation emptied my girth.

Breaching a new land comes with some doubt,
but it wasn't the ocean that choked us out.

～

It wasn't the ocean that choked us out
in thoughtless gray waves of churning rage
but sluicing land atop shoreline redoubt,
our newest home a wasteland—death's raw stage.

If there was a healer who could touch the sky
and dry up the heavens, our only roof,
I would call her to task for watching us die
like animals, bent crosses our only proof.

In good faith we arrived to scatter Black seed
rejoin lost tribes of ancient kings and queens;
among us would arise a new kind to lead,
build, trade, birth, becoming people of means.

Not needing letters home begging for more:
our tools, our land, our food all on home shores.

≈

Our tools, our land, our food all on home shores,
we recall the flavor of our freedman's song,
the will to survive wrapped in meager stores
and the prayers of the hearty lifting our throng.

Reaching our destination, a low sunken place,
unfanned by breezes, a stagnant bay,
and endless water and vegetable waste.
Hearts suddenly broken, mouths with few words to say.

The rain and the water used with purpose
bring disease and malady without cessation.
Our fearful cries soon turn to vile curses
and rancor at being forced to leave our nation.

America refit ships to carry us,
trading slave whips for Bibles and malaria.

# Home Again

The Nation has not yet found peace from its sins; the freedman has not yet found in freedom his promised land.

 —W. E. B. Du Bois, *The Souls of Black Folk*

# Reconstruction

Slavery ended with the Civil War when
armed troops lockstepped with federal law
in defense of liberty's new geography.

The Freedman's Bureau replacing whips &
chains with indenture for the underage,
a civil bondage for the once enslaved.

Polly, not yet eighteen, became an apprentice,
mistress of skills that would soon earn wages.
Crisp bills freedom's new cartography.

Others gained a pittance for toil,
once done for free, if you discount bones bent
by slavery's war of hunger & disease.

The mansion on the hill yet beckoned &
slave quarters still housed the newly freed,
ownership indeed an out-of-reach geography.

Freedom tempered by debt and low wages
distrust between broken masters and broke slaves
despite a civil war to end bond slavery:
this was proud liberty's sly geography.

# Just in Case They Change Their Minds, Let My Epitaph Read, *Free*

*for my great-grandfather William G. Hairston, b. 1865*

What could they do after the war
to grow a fear, making you change
a birth date the year the Union held sway
and rebels stomped boots to say
the South will rise again, ascend
like yeast, lofty with disdain,
raising red, white, and blue,
malleable hues, to offend and exclude.
How you arose from refuse,
swaybacked shack, of splintered pine
coming off that land
owned by Scotsmen with a plan
to stay out of spite and rapturously
rewrite post-Emancipation life.
Smiles above saffron buttercups
yanked from soil and held under chins
shining like butter to reveal those
who married to keep their skin
and those who wed to wash it black again.
Three years past Appomattox
and freedmen being forced
from casting their votes, pushing Blacks

off plantations so they had no home.
We weren't important until it was clear
Confederates didn't want
Ulysses S. Grant as president.
Hundreds of freedmen died in Georgia
before and after the '68 election,
stark Black voter intimidation,
bodies in trees and filled with holes
made it clear the Fourteenth and Fifteenth Amendments
had to hold in a restitched nation
or suffer destruction
without a Black vote solution.

# Up from Slavery

My great-grandfather kept the peace / between the races
a man of two faces / qualified, after being born a slave
to rectify and demystify / the role of Black men / before
the throes of white sin. / Post-Reconstruction, to stay alive
raise eight children / with his wife / all at the same time.
A religious man / in the way Blacks fell on Jesus / when hate
fell on them / like white on rice / or white on raisins. / Call it
charisma / he charisma'd between Black and white / even
in his photograph / square-jaw handsome / dissonance
between coat, tie, and well-worn shoes / hint of a wedding
ring knuckled from view. / A blond forelock brushed into
tawny waves / any old-time Hollywood lead might crave.

# A Meditation on the Toppling of the Confederate Statue *Silent Sam*

*University of North Carolina Campus, 1913–2018*

Sun-glazed statue too hot to climb
little orphaned rebel whistling
the Old South will rise. Collective whiplash,

when a woman lies sprawled beneath a grill;
in Charlottesville Nazis bear gruesome grins.
Sun-glazed statue too hot to climb

cooked up in America's kitchen over time.
The metonymy of warfare: a lad and gun,
a whiplashed slave, the Old South's son.

From the stairs of the Wilson Library
I spy ribbons of *Do Not Cross* tape
and one less sun-glazed statue to climb.

I reopen a sealed wound, the files of slavery,
each day a reckoning with ancestry
and whip-smart visions of the Old South's demise.

More news of another blackface moment,
Virginia gov'ner caught culturally misspoken.
Sun-glazed statues circumventing time
still taunting freedom with *the Old South will rise.*

# Slivers

Deoxy-
ribonucleic
acid
DNA
building block
of genomes
1% anomaly
making
humans
individuals.
Ninety-nine
percent
of fabric
identical
except for
a sliver
of disparity
enough
to propagate
antipathy
toward
Black skin
coiled pate
bridgeless nose
darkest
brown

iris
orbiting pupil
indelible
somatic
crime.
In biology
never asked
to consider
how little
difference
racial
distinction
makes
in the
tonal scheme
of the
human race
this diffusion
this sliver
of recessive
inspiration.

# Afterword

# My African American Sensibility Speaks to My Scottish Genes about the Miniseries *Outlander*

I did not stay up to pen a poem
while screening Scottish history
slipshod neo-porn
with unaccented moans.
This series has got me going
five episodes a day
no end in sight
just me working to justify
lost hours of my life.
I'm not kidding myself, nor do I believe
these kilted men are kin to me.
They drink whiskey at every turn
betwixt and between wars
gory knife assaults and corded whip scars.
When Jamie says *Claire*, it gurgles like a curse
way back in his throat
as if he might end up
with spittle spraying from his mouth.
Then there's the ubiquitous red hair—
daughter Brianna more persimmon
than her pumpkin spice progenitor.
*I hate these characters*, my brain rails,

yet I've grown used to seeing
Jamie's tight arse and Claire's 34Bs
and the way they lunge at each other
at the end of every other scene.
Still, if I hear one more uttered
*bairn* or *kin ta ya* . . .
I don't know what I might do.
And no one, not one of them,
bathes enough for me.

# Acknowledgments

The author wishes to thank the following for publishing versions of select poems in this collection:

*Banyan Review,* "Dear Ancestors: On the Occasion of Visiting the Plantation Which Once Governed Your Lives"

*Birmingham Poetry Review,* "Hemings Family Tour"

*Cutleaf,* "An Extant Slave Receipt Signed *Peter Hairston,*" "Encroachment," "Every Day Can Be Resistance," and "Of Bison and Bullets: A Preservation Project"

*Green Mountains Review,* "A Bondage Nocturne" (including the portion originally published as "Branching") and "A Meditation on the Toppling of the Confederate Statue *Silent Sam*"

*James Dickey Review,* "Racial Ambiguity"

*Kweli,* "A Creased Page from a Hairston Plantation Ledger"

*Pangyrus,* "Afterword: My African American Sensibility Speaks to My Scottish Genes about the Miniseries *Outlander*"

*Poetry,* "Crops: Tobacco," "Resurrection," "Pancakes Keep Coming to Mind: A Sestina Commemorating the Demise of Aunt Jemima on the Pancake Box," and a portion of "A Bondage Nocturne" originally published as "Tradition: A Perilous Time in a Black Girl's Life"

*Salamander,* "Up from Slavery"

*Scoundrel Time,* "What I Will and Will Not Take from a Planter Ancestor"

*Solstice,* "Plantation Aubade: Freedom as Lover" and "Severed: A Statement on the Ludicrous Nature of African Repatriation"

*Tahoma Literary Review,* "Matrilineal"

*The Rumpus*, "A Black Doe in the Anthropocene" and "Runners: A Ghazal for Our Times"

*Why I Wrote This Poem: 62 Poets on Creating Their Works*, "Vibrio Cholerae"

The original slavery-era texts that are transcribed in full in "Runaway Slave Affidavit Dated March 1831" and "The Negro Girl Letter" and quoted elsewhere are used by permission and are located in the Wilson and Hairston Family Papers #04134, Southern Historical Collection, Wilson Library, the University of North Carolina at Chapel Hill. Any errors are the sole responsibility of the author.

## Deepest Gratitude

This book would not have been possible without the generous support of the following people and institutions. Many thanks to Albright College and a faculty development research grant I received in the summer of 2018 while I served as National Endowment for the Humanities visiting professor of American studies. This grant allowed me to make my initial research trip to the University of North Carolina at Chapel Hill to review the Wilson and Hairston Family Papers. The grant was followed by a summer 2023 Faculty Development and Research "Grow It" Grant sponsored by East Stroudsburg University that enabled me to travel to Ghana. While in Ghana, I collected cultural and experiential data to document my African return journey and to enhance the story of the once enslaved who emigrated to Africa in the nineteenth century in search of true racial equity. I am also grateful for the time to write and to share work in a supportive community of writers provided by residencies from the Sewanee Writers' Conference and the Bread Loaf Writers' Conference. Many thanks to the anonymous peer readers of this manuscript and the board of trustees of the University Press of Kentucky for their unanimous endorsement for publication, to senior acquisitions editor Abby Freeland for her utmost support, and to copyeditor Iris A. Law.

# Notes

## *Foreword*

King, Martin Luther Jr. "I Have a Dream." *A Call to Conscience: The Landmark Speeches of Dr. Martin Luther King, Jr.*, edited by Clayborne Carson and Kris Shepard, IPM, Intellectual Properties Management, in association with Warner Books, 2001, p. 82.

## *Original Sin*

Part epigraphs

Whitfield, James M. "America." *The Norton Anthology of African American Literature*, edited by Henry Louis Gates Jr. and Nellie Y. McKay, 2nd ed., W. W. Norton & Company, 2004, p. 484.

Jacobs, Harriet A. *Incidents in the Life of a Slave Girl, Written by Herself.* 1861. Edited by Koritha Mitchell, Broadview Press, 2023, p. 117.

"A Bondage Nocturne" is a versed response to my great-great-grandmother Mima's story of being impregnated at age fourteen. These documented cases made me think more pointedly about female coming-of-age enslavement narratives. I have always experienced dismay reading Harriet Jacobs's heartbreaking story, but even her poignant account left me unprepared for birth dates indicating the assembly-line tactics of planters and overseers impregnating young girls on plantations. The penultimate section of the poem refers obliquely to Mima and specifically to "Yellow" Milly, a fellow enslaved girl who was impregnated at fifteen and gave birth to her first child at sixteen. Mima, like Milly, was biracial, which also indicates that their

79

mothers were used by planters and/or overseers as "breeders"—a fate that their daughters then inherited. Important birthdates for Mima and Milly were pulled from Hairston, Peter W., *The Cooleemee Plantation and Its People.* Hunter Publishing Company, 1986.

The final section of the poem "Hemings Family Tour" contains a reference to Kentucky author Gayl Jones and was inspired by her important novel *Corregidora*, which is the story of multiple generations of women in a family being fathered by the same planter master.

The poem "An Extant Slave Receipt Signed *Peter Hairston*" (1777) is based on a slave receipt, dated 1777, I uncovered in the Wilson and Hairston Family Papers #04134, Southern Historical Collection, Wilson Library, the University of North Carolina at Chapel Hill. The sale of a mother and child by Peter Hairston was carried out by an agent on behalf of Mrs. Mary Byrd. It appears that Mrs. Byrd was the purchaser of the two, which later brought to mind this quote from Stephanie E. Jones-Rogers's recent book on the role of white women as enslavers: "For them, slavery was their freedom. They created freedom for themselves by actively engaging and investing in the economy of slavery and keeping African Americans in captivity."
Jones-Rogers, Stephanie E. *They Were Her Property: White Women as Slave Owners in the American South.* Yale UP, 2020, p. xvii.

On June 17, 2020 Quaker Oats announced that it would remove the image of Aunt Jemima from its pancake boxes. This move was motivated by the year's wanton killing of Black men and women by police. "Pancakes Keep Coming to Mind: A Sestina Commemorating the Demise of Aunt Jemima on the Pancake Box" was inspired by the imagery that I could not shake from my mind after learning that my great-great-grandmother's name was Mima. The truncated form of the name constantly brought to mind Aunt Jemima because of her iconic commercialization.

"A Creased Page from a Hairston Plantation Ledger" is based on an archived slave roll with a price list of human property belonging to the Hairstons. The poem documents my deeply felt connection to these human beings (some undoubtedly relatives) who comprised this list, and my speculation about their nineteenth-century lives in and near Davie and Stokes counties, North Carolina. The text of this list is contained in the Wilson and Hairston Family Papers #04134, Southern Historical Collection, Wilson Library, the University of North Carolina at Chapel Hill.

The found poem "Runaway Slave Affidavit" is a full transcription of an actual testimony given to a local Virginia magistrate. The testimony identifies runaway property belonging to the planter Robert Hairston. The original text of the notice is contained in the Wilson and Hairston Family Papers #04134, Southern Historical Collection, Wilson Library, the University of North Carolina at Chapel Hill.

The poem "Resurrection" begins with a historical note detailing Nat Turner's Rebellion.
Turner, Nat. *The Confessions of Nat Turner, the Leader of the Late Insurrection in Southampton, Virginia*. 1831. Edited by Thomas R. Gray, e-book, the University of North Carolina Press, 2011, p. 5.

The epigraph before the poem "George's Dilemma Anno Domini 1777" is taken from a court-ordered request for planter Peter Hairston's enslaved man, George, to carry a weapon, which was illegal for enslaved Black people to do. The text of the notice is contained in the Wilson and Hairston Family Papers # 04134, Southern Historical Collection, Wilson Library, the University of North Carolina at Chapel Hill. The timing of the request was just after the signing of the Declaration of Independence, when British soldiers were still engaged in tactical battles in the US, especially in the South. Additionally, in 1775, Virginia governor Lord Dunsmore issued a proclamation freeing any Virginia

*81*

indentured servant or "Negro" slave who took up arms alongside the British.

*Vibrio cholerae* is the Latin genus and species for the bacteria that causes the disease cholera. The epigraph before the poem "Vibrio Cholerae" is taken from a letter that documents a delay in travel to Liberia of a group of Black Hairstons from Norfolk, Virginia. The letter is contained in the Wilson and Hairston Family Papers #04134, Southern Historical Collection, Wilson Library, the University of North Carolina at Chapel Hill.

"My Father Singing 'John Henry'"

*The History of Mary Prince, A West Indian Slave.* 1831. *The Classic Slave Narratives*, edited and with an updated introduction by Henry Louis Gates Jr., Signet Classics, 1987, 2012, p. 238.

de Crèvecœur, J. Hector St. John. *Letters from an American Farmer and Sketches of Eighteenth-Century America.* 1782. Edited with an introduction by Albert E. Stone, Penguin Books, 1963, 1981, p. 177.

The found poem "The Negro Girl Letter" comprises the full text of an actual letter from Mr. Geremiah to Peter Hairston regarding a slave rental. The letter also provides a glimpse into enslavement's physical toll on the Black body. The context of the letter deals with the practice of slave rentals between planters when extra hands or skilled labor was needed. Though probably not the case in this instance, rental was a common practice among people who could not afford to keep a large number of enslaved persons. The original letter is contained in the Wilson and Hairston Family Papers # 04134, Southern Historical Collection, Wilson Library, The University of North Carolina at Chapel Hill.

The title of the poem "Esclave/Schiava/Escrava/Slave" comprises translations of the word *slave* into Spanish, Italian, and Portuguese.

*82*

## Back to Africa

Part epigraph

Ayers, E. "American Colonization Society." Western Recorder. *Methodist Magazine.* vol. 7, Nov. 1824, pp. 417–20. *American Antiquarian Society (AAS) Historical Periodicals Collection: Series 2,* p. 420. https:// web-p-ebscohost-com.proxyesu.klnpa.org/ehost/archiveviewer /archive?vid=2&sid=347169fb-f2d7-411a-98aa-96aaac77f213%40re dis&bdata=JnNpdGU9ZWhvc3QtbGl2ZQ%3d%3d#kw=true&acc =false&lpId=NA&ppId=divp17&twPV=&xOff=0&yOff=0&zm=fi t&fs=&rot=0&docMapOpen=true&pageMapOpen=true&AN= 44885885&db=h9i. Accessed 7 December 2024.

"Severed: A Statement on the Ludicrous Nature of African Repatriation" contains a detailed reference to Emperor Sundiata, a foundational hero of the African nation of Mali.

"The Vanishing" references the serendipitous discovery of potter Thomas Commeraw's true race. According to a New York Historical Society exhibit placard, "The 1800 Federal Census counted Commeraw and the 7 members of his household. The census taker listed him as Black. It was this detail, discovered by a researcher in 2003, that overturned the long-held assumption that Commeraw was a white craftsman."

Commeraw, Thomas. *Crafting Freedom: The Life and Legacy of Free Black Potter Thomas W. Commeraw.* 27 Jan.–28 May 2023, The New York Historical, New York.

The poems "The Origins of an 'Americo' in Liberia," "Vibrio Cholerae," "The Vanishing," "Homegoing to Africa as Ars Poetica," and "Sherbro, West Africa" deal with the history of Black American repatriation to Africa under the auspices of the American Colonization Society in the nineteenth century. The project was not a benevolent one, but was a methodology for removing the "problem" of free Black people from the American landscape. Many thousands of free and recently freed African Americans emigrated to West Africa, frequently under the sponsorship of past masters and mistresses. What they often found were difficult living conditions and sickness from diseases that were not endemic to the US. Many migrants died soon after arrival, and others made the decision to return to the US. Those who stayed built lives around the values they brought with them from America to the continent of Africa. These values culturally set them apart from Indigenous Africans and earned them the moniker "Americoes," a term used in Ciment, James. *Another America: The Story of Liberia and the Former Slaves Who Ruled It*. Hill and Wang, 2013.

## *Home Again*
Part epigraph

Du Bois, W. E. B. *The Souls of Black Folk*. 1903. Edited with an introduction by David W. Blight and Robert Gooding-Williams, Bedford Books, 1997, p. 40.

# About the Author

Christopher Descano

Artress Bethany White is a poet, essayist, and literary critic. She is the recipient of the 2018 Trio Award for her collection *My Afmerica: Poems*, selected by poet Sun Yung Shin. Her prose collection, *Survivor's Guilt: Essays on Race and American Identity*, received a 2022 Next Generation Finalist Indie Book Award. She is associate professor of English at East Stroudsburg University and coeditor of the anthology *Wheatley at 250: Black Women Poets Re-imagine the Verse of Phillis Wheatley Peters.*